# Making Faces

## Jacob DC Ross

ISBN: 0996147802
ISBN-13: 978-0-9961478-0-4

## Dedication

For Amy and Ella, and for all the people, neurotypical or on the spectrum, from whom I draw inspiration and support.

# For Parents and Educators

I wrote this book with the intent of helping you and the children with whom you work. Difficulty with or the inability to naturally recognize emotions based on facial expressions is a serious hindrance to social development. If children on the autism spectrum practice and memorize facial expressions, they can learn to respond better to non-verbal cues from their conversation partner.

You can allow your child or students to read this book on their own. You might find that you get better results if you sit down with the child and read it together. If they have any questions about the various facial expressions, you'll be in a position to help them. You can use the various pages as flash cards. Each picture page faces the page that names the emotion displayed by the model. Just show your child the picture, ask them what the name of the emotion is and what are the clues to the model's expressions.

I sincerely hope that you and your children enjoy a deepened bond and that they see improvements in their relationships with other autistic children and neurotypical kids as a result of working with this book. I'm a man living with Asperger syndrome, and I understand the difficulty that children can face in their interactions with others when emotional cues aren't apparent.

Many thanks,
Jacob DC Ross

What face is this?

See how her mouth turns up at the corners?

Look how her eyes are raised up and slightly closed.

This person is HAPPY!

Happy people smile a lot.

A smile shows in your mouth and in your eyes.

Why not try smiling when you talk to people?

What face is this?

See how they hold their hand?

Notice their turned-down mouth and eyes.

This person is SAD.

People turn their eyes and mouth down when they aren't happy.

Touching their head like that means they are very sad.

When you can see that someone's sad, ask them what's wrong and what you can do to help.

What face is this?

See how her head is tilted forward.

Her eyes are slightly closed and she's not smiling.

6

This person is MAD!

People focus their eyes on you when they are angry.

Lips pinched together tightly means they're annoyed.

When someone is mad at you apologize, and ask why they're angry.

What face is this?

Her eyes and mouth are open wide.

Her head is tilted back.

This person is SCARED!

People tilt their head away from what scares them.

They open their eyes wide and gasp.

If someone is scared you might need to ask a grown-up for help.

What face is this?

Notice the tension in her mouth and eyes.

See how she holds her lipstick.

This person is UNCOMFORTABLE.

Her smile is wide, but her eyes don't look happy.

If people play with things while you talk they are probably distracted.

If someone is uncomfortable while you talk, give them a chance to talk instead.

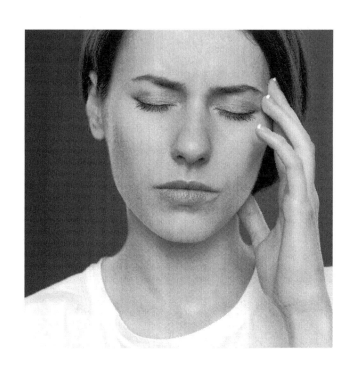

What face is this?

Notice that her eyes are closed.

See how she touches her face?

This person is IN PAIN.

People close their eyes and don't smile when they hurt.

Sometimes folks touch where it hurts to make it feel better.

When someone is in pain, ask them what you can do to help.

13

What face is this?

Notice her smile.

See how her eyes are open wide?

This person is SURPRISED!

Surprised people smile with their mouth open.

Wide eyes mean they really like what they see.

If someone looks surprised they are probably happy about something you did.

What face is this?

Notice where her eyes are looking.

See how she touches her mouth?

This person is DISTRACTED.

People look at what interests them.

Touching your lips means that you are thinking deeply.

If someone is distracted, ask what they are looking at or let them go do what they need to do.

What face is this?

See how her eybrows are crinkled?

Look at how she touches her mouth.

This person is CONFUSED.

Her eyebrow position and the finger on her mouth means she is thinking deeply.

Her eyes show you that she doesn't understand something.

When someone is confused, ask what they don't understand and try to repeat what you've been saying in a new way.

What face is this?


Notice how her eyes look right at you.


What does it mean when you touch your lips?

This person is INTERESTED.

Narrowed eyes mean she is only looking at you right now.

Her finger on the lips shows you she is thinking about what you say.

When someone is interested in what you're saying, it means they want to hear more from you.

What face is this?

Do you see her big smile?

Notice how her eyebrows go up.

This person is EXCITED!

Wide eyes and a big smile are good clues.

Excited people jump up and down sometimes.

When someone is excited, let them talk so they can tell you what they want to say.

What face is this?

Look how her finger points straight up.

See how her lips are puckered?

This person wants you to be QUIET.

A finger straight up over the mouth means you're being too loud.

Sometimes people say things that they shouldn't tell other people.

When someone asks you to be quiet, whisper and ask them why and if it's okay to talk softly, or if you have to not talk at all.

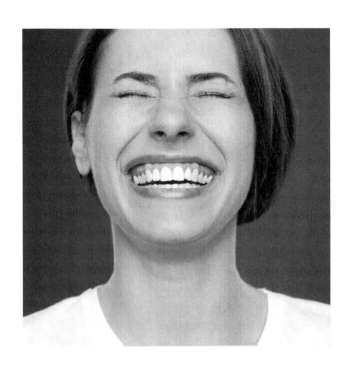

What face is this?

See how her head is thrown back?

Notice her large smile.

This person is LAUGHING!

People smile, throw back their heads and sometimes close their eyes when they laugh.

Laughing can be loud, but it means that they are happy, not mad or sad.

When someone is laughing and you don't know why, ask what's funny so you can laugh too!

## About the Author

Jacob DC Ross is a
lifelong Oregonian and
an Aspie. He resides in
Portland with his family.

Made in the USA
San Bernardino, CA
16 September 2016